JIM HARRISON

THE THEORY
& PRACTICE
OF RIVERS

Edited by Joseph Bednarik
Introduction by Rebecca Solnit

COPPER CANYON PRESS
PORT TOWNSEND, WASHINGTON

Cover art: Russell Chatham, *Armstrong Spring Creek*, 1985.
Oil on canvas, 20 × 16 inches.

Copper Canyon Press is in residence at Fort Worden State Park in Port Townsend, Washington, under the auspices of Centrum. Centrum is a gathering place for artists and creative thinkers from around the world, students of all ages and backgrounds, and audiences seeking extraordinary cultural enrichment.

Editor's Note: In stanza three of the poem "What He Said When I Was Eleven," there is a factual error. St. Basil's Cathedral is located in Moscow, not Leningrad (St. Petersburg). If Jim were alive, I would ask him to make the correction. While I am humbled that this error slipped past me in previous publications, I am grateful to proofreader Marie Landau for setting the record straight. —JB

LIBRARY OF CONGRESS CATALOGING-IN-PUBLICATION DATA

Names: Harrison, Jim, 1937–2016, author. | Bednarik, Joseph, 1964– editor. | Solnit, Rebecca, writer of introduction.
Title: The theory & practice of rivers / Jim Harrison ; edited by Joseph Bednarik ; introduction by Rebecca Solnit.
Other titles: The theory & practice of rivers and new poems | The theory and practice of rivers
Description: Port Townsend, Washington : Copper Canyon Press, 2025. | Summary: "A collection of poems by Jim Harrison"— Provided by publisher.
Identifiers: LCCN 2024047903 (print) | LCCN 2024047904 (ebook) | ISBN 9781556597183 (paperback) | ISBN 9781556597138 (hardcover) | ISBN 9781619323117 (epub)
Subjects: LCGFT: Poetry.
Classification: LCC PS3558.A67 T48 2025 (print) | LCC PS3558.A67 (ebook) | DDC 811/.54—dc23/eng/20241101
LC record available at https://lccn.loc.gov/2024047903
LC ebook record available at https://lccn.loc.gov/2024047904

9 8 7 6 5 4 3 2 FIRST PRINTING

COPPER CANYON PRESS
Post Office Box 271
Port Townsend, Washington 98368
www.coppercanyonpress.org

THE THEORY &
PRACTICE OF RIVERS

BOOKS BY JIM HARRISON

POETRY COLLECTIONS

Plain Song

Locations

Outlyer & Ghazals

Letters to Yesenin

Returning to Earth

Selected & New Poems, 1961–1981

The Theory & Practice of Rivers
    and New Poems

After Ikkyū & Other Poems

The Shape of the Journey:
    New & Collected Poems

Braided Creek: A Conversation
    in Poetry, with Ted Kooser

Saving Daylight

In Search of Small Gods

Songs of Unreason

Dead Man's Float

The Essential Poems

Collected Ghazals

Complete Poems

NONFICTION

Just Before Dark: Collected Nonfiction

The Raw and the Cooked: Adventures
    of a Roving Gourmand

Off to the Side: A Memoir

A Really Big Lunch: The Roving
    Gourmand on Food and Life

The Search for the Genuine:
    Nonfiction, 1970–2015

NOVELS

Wolf: A False Memoir

A Good Day to Die

Farmer

Warlock

Sundog

Dalva

The Road Home

True North

Returning to Earth

The English Major

The Great Leader

The Big Seven

NOVELLA COLLECTIONS

Legends of the Fall

The Woman Lit by Fireflies

Julip

The Beast God Forgot to Invent

The Summer He Didn't Die

The Farmer's Daughter

The River Swimmer

Brown Dog

The Ancient Minstrel

CHILDREN'S

The Boy Who Ran to the Woods

In Memoriam
Gloria Ellen Harrison
1964–1979

In a life properly lived, you're a river.

Jim Harrison

CONTENTS

THE GOSPEL ACCORDING TO WATER

Rebecca Solnit

The long poem that takes up most of this book could be called many things, an elegy for his niece dead at sixteen, a loose memoir in which Harrison recounts various experiences he's had and places he's been (and also, in one aria of ingredients, what he's cooking), as well as what adds up to a list of rivers and another of girls and women. But it never stops being a poem. By which I mean that it offers what I as a prose writer go to poetry to find, again and again: a reminder that language doesn't have to proceed step by step, by rational argument, but can take intuitive leaps from one subject to another, navigate by association rather than build an argument the way you build a brick wall, liberate itself even from the limits of language to indicate what lies beneath and beyond, and trust the reader to follow, or go where it will with those readers who have leaps in them too.

If I read nothing but news stories and scientific reports and tweets about politics, the language in which I think and write can trudge along carrying its informational loads like a mule in a packtrain or up-armor itself to win arguments. Poetry reminds me to take flight like a bird, to drop some of the burdens and navigate another way, to seek other less tangible, quantifiable goods, though even that makes it sound practical and transactional. Let me start again: Mostly I read poetry for a particular kind of pleasure that includes the beauty of imagery and language that is inseparable from the power of insight and unexpected perspectives.

Good poetry awakens, opens doors, charts routes that logic cannot, invites me to open up to my own imagination and my own ear for the music of language and to live and write from that deeper, wilder self. Jim Harrison has long been one of the poets I turn to, and a paperback copy of an earlier edition of this book, bought used (the $8 in pencil is still on the flyleaf), has accompanied me on various journeys across the Southwest.

Harrison's poetry reminds me that it's when our species is most social, most caught up in the purely human or rather in a conventional version of our humanity, that it loses sight of the reality of both the body and the world beyond the human. The social is a kind of sandbar you get stranded on, out of the flow of these other things. What gets called the spiritual is often revealed through the natural: you go deep to go high, go out—out of the self, out of the house, out of city limits—to go inward. Or you find a version of self that includes the biological and the metaphysical or yearnings for same.

Harrison washes up in the social a fair amount—the title poem is mostly about rivers and women he cares about, but it also stops in Los Angeles and in New York City (where, he grouses, he goes to a party "where very rich people / talked about their arches"). But he was lucky to be raised in a rural place in which the presence of animals and the primordial forces of weather, seasons, and water were strong, and we are lucky that he returns again and again to these beings and forces and places. His poetry is rich with revelations of and through the nonhuman.

This poem, one of Harrison's longest, meanders. *Meander* is a verb for what both rivers and people sometimes do, moving aimlessly or erratically, and the word comes from a Greek name for a god who was a river and a river who was a god. The lower stretch of that river twists and turns across what's now Turkey, so there's also a subway station in Istanbul that carries one version of the river's name. You can float down a god, drink a little of him, or stand on the platform that is the god waiting for your train. Harrison writes in "The Theory & Practice of Rivers":

But this isn't a map of the gods.
When they live in rivers
it's because rivers have no equilibrium;
gods resent equilibrium when everything
that lives *moves*

We are all verbs in drag as nouns. Everything is. Stripping away this disguise, this delusion, freeing us to move, is a goal and task that runs all through his poetry. As his editor Joseph Bednarik observes in his prefatory note to the *Complete Poems*, among the most frequently used words in them are *god, bird,* and *river.* This holy trinity tends to show up in his work as incarnations or emblems of moments of freedom, awareness, full presence, vehicles of transformation—not so much transformation into something else but release into the ceaseless transformation of being. Or awakening to the true nature of being. This poem tells us that

> I forgot where I heard that poems
> are designed to waken sleeping gods

The gods Harrison is forever invoking are not so much deities in the usual sense but those occasions of deep awareness in which, as William Wordswoth, another poet in love with the nonhuman world, wandering, epiphany, and informal language, put it,

> While with an eye made quiet by the power
> Of harmony, and the deep power of joy,
> We see into the life of things.

In such encounters, we leave behind the self-absorption, the distraction, the practical business, see beyond ourselves into something deeper and truer, get out of the self and its clinging and attachment and into the ceaselessly changing world. This letting go to fully enter the river of time is the divine flashing up, unpredictably, ephemerally. In Harrison's poems, the gods are the moment, the perception, ourselves lit up by the fire of realization, presence itself, immanence rather than transcendence. We let go of the trap of our noun identity and flow as verbs. "Moving water is forever in the present tense, a condition we rather achingly avoid," Harrison writes in the opening page of his memoir *Off to the Side.*

Other belief systems emphasize the immortality of the gods and conflate that with changelessness, but Harrison's are gods of change, gods who live in rivers, who are rivers, who are liquid not solid, verbs not nouns, being not beings, the thoughts and not the thinker. These gods are against equilibrium and they remind us that everything *moves.* These gods are change itself. This is where his love of rivers and his attention to the theory and practice of Buddhism, particularly Zen Buddhism, meet. To put it in river language, they come to a confluence here.

Someone once shamefacedly asked Shunryu Suzuki Roshi, the founder of San Francisco Zen Center, one of the great portals for Soto Zen in the West, if he could condense zen down to a sentence. Without missing a beat, Suzuki Roshi replied, "Everything changes." Transience, impermanence are central to Buddhist teaching and so is being in the here and now—what you could call the present tense. This is why the gods resent equilibrium: As an attempt, it dams up the flow of change; as an ideal, it opposes the mutability of all things.

I've called the title poem a memoir and an elegy; I could also call it a sermon. Harrison once told an interviewer, "Up to sixteen I wanted to be a preacher, and then one day I did a whirlwind: I jumped from Jesus to John Keats in three days." He mostly left the church behind, so far as I can tell, but not preaching, as the poem "Homily" in this volume reminds us. A good many of his poems give admonitions and instructions, though given his passion for place, landscape, and hedonism, maybe they could be described as directions: "Don't go there, it sucks; but up on that ridge is something wonderful if not so easy to get to."

And mostly he preaches the gospel according to water. "Gods resent equilibrium when everything that lives *moves*" is a line worth repeating, and in another of his countless interviews he declared, "In a life properly lived, you're a river. You touch things lightly or deeply; you move along because life herself moves, and you can't stop it; you can't figure out a banal game plan applicable to all situations; you just have to go with the 'beingness' of life, as Rilke would have it. In *Sundog,* Strang says a dam doesn't stop a river, it just controls the flow. Technically speaking, you can't stop one at all." In his 1973 novel *A*

Good Day to Die, three passionate though ill-prepared "ecoterrorists" conspire to blow up a dam.*

In preparation for writing this introduction, I wanted to read the title poem unbroken—every time I got to the bottom of a page I felt like I'd hit a dam that broke its flow. So with the help of the publisher's PDF, I printed out "The Theory & Practice of Rivers," and trimmed the pages and taped them together into a continuous scroll about sixteen feet long, a river of words I could travel through freely. It helped. As I plied scissors and tape, the Yurok and other tribes on the Klamath River in far Northern California were spearheading the biggest dam removal project this country has yet seen, freeing four hundred miles of river for chinook and coho salmon, steelhead, and other fish to travel freely, as they once did. The river's liberation resulted from seeing it as a living system, not just a power generator or water resource, from seeing the verb of it more than the noun, and out of settler society finally listening to the first stewards of these fish, these waters, this land. For a river, which could be defined as water falling downhill, equilibrium might mean the stagnant water behind dams, the imprisonment or drowning of flow.

The more we believe we are nouns the more we believe in stability, objectivity, ownership, control, permanence. *River* is a noun but a good case could be made that it's a verb, and in Mojave poet Natalie Diaz's long poem "The First Water Is the Body," she affirms this, writing, "I mean *river* as a verb. A happening. It is moving within me right now." She describes the inseparability of her people, them from their river, the stretch of the lower Colorado as it approaches

---

*Here I could remark that I did not love that novel and that I prefer Harrison's poetry to his fiction and nonfiction. Unlike some of the authors of introductions to the new Copper Canyon releases of Harrison's books of poems, I never met him, and that might have been a good thing, since we might have hit it off, or might have annoyed each other mightily. I'm not thrilled by the lines in "Homily" later in this book: "don't read / dirty magazines in front of stewardesses" and "don't fall in love / with photos of ladies in magazines" that presume a straight male reader. But I'm grateful for what Harrison had to give that it's been helpful or joyful to receive, and that he could write "And maybe I could describe the cages in which my heroines lived because as a male I unconsciously helped to build those cages."

the Gulf of Mexico. "I carry a river. It is who I am: 'Aha Makav. This is not metaphor."

Most of us carry a river, though without the spiritual and moral engagement and awareness of the Mojave and Diaz's particular subgroup, the Gila River Indian Community. I grew up a little north of the Golden Gate Bridge on Coast Miwok territory, drinking water mostly from the Russian River; I've spent most of my adult life on Ramaytush Ohlone territory on the bridge's south side, which means I'm mostly made out of water from the Tuolumne River, much of which in turn begins as snowmelt from the storms blown in from the Pacific.

A river is a verb, everything is a river, and rivers do not exist as stable entities; water is forever entering and exiting what a cartographer would describe as a river, and a Confucian saying reminds us that pure water has no fish. Along with water, the contents of a river include ever-changing sediment, plants, decaying dead things, and myriad living beings from the one-celled plankton and algae to the moose I once saw grazing placidly on the bottom of the fast-moving Tuchodi in the Canadian Rockies, its legs splayed to brace against the powerful current.

A river is also its route across the land, but these too shift and migrate, as I found in 2021 when I and my collaborators, the photographers Mark Klett and Byron Wolfe, spent three days on the banks of the Merced in Yosemite Valley looking for the exact location from which Eadweard Muybridge took a photograph in 1872. Eventually we realized the river had not only been flowing west all this time but it had also migrated north about a hundred feet to settle in a new bed. The Mississippi has famously had many routes to the Gulf, and preventing it from shifting again has been the goal of massive hydraulic engineering projects over the past century, and the Rio Grande has been defined as the US-Mexico border in its lower stretches, but it has a habit of throwing out a new oxbow or otherwise shifting its bed, forever undermining the desire that it be synonymous with a fixed and permanent divide.

We're rivers in that an unceasing stream of stuff and information is entering us, a nonstop stream of other stuff is leaving us—all that secretion and excretion that living bodies generate, maybe also the occasional baby for those among the uterus-equipped, and otherwise the fruit of our labors, in that lovely old phrase, be it carpentry or poetry or clean floors in the cafeteria. What we think of as our bodily selves are compilations: More than half the cells in our bodies are not human, not possessed of "our" DNA. We are plural, thanks to the billions of microbes that are essential parts of our functioning. We are crossroads, ecosystems, pumping stations, congregations lumbering along together; we are rivers.*

The preposterous idea of self-sufficiency ignores that no one gives birth to themselves and everyone constantly takes in lungsful of the atmosphere that lies like an ethereal dermis over the entire surface of the earth. We can only live minutes without oxygen, days without water, weeks without the food that is other living beings. We are verbs in drag as nouns, processes with delusions of permanence, fluids pretending to be solids, since we're two-thirds water, our skin a sack to hold it in. "Time is a river that snatches me away," wrote Jorge Luis Borges, "but I am the river." In Harrison's elegy for a dead child, time is the river that has dragged her away; becoming that river is a way to reclaim her or reconcile with the loss.

A river is motion, is water forever entering and exiting it, coming from springs, snowmelt, tributaries, going into larger rivers the way the Virgin River mentioned in this poem goes into the Colorado, or into the sea the way other rivers mentioned here, the Nile, the Amazon, and the Mississippi, do, while the Salt River flows into the Gila which flows into the Colorado, as does the San Juan, into which the

*In the remarkable essay "A Manifesto for a Processual Philosophy of Biology," John Dupré and Daniel J. Nicholson write, "From a metabolic perspective, it is simply a matter of fact that, in an organism, *everything flows*. . . . Overall, the reality of metabolism forces us to recognize that organisms, despite their apparent fixity and solidity, are not material things but fluid processes; they are metabolic streams of matter and energy that exhibit dynamic stabilities relative to particular timescales. As processes, and unlike things or substances, organisms have to undergo constant change to continue to be the entities that they are." From *Everything Flows: Towards a Processual Philosophy of Biology* (Oxford Academic, 2018).

del Muerto fork mentioned here flows via Chinle Creek. "Water is life" said the Lakota organizers at Standing Rock protesting the fossil-fuel pipeline, and water is forever moving, metamorphosing, evaporating up into the sky, falling out of it as rain and snow. Affirming this impermanence as truth and delight happens over and over in Harrison's work.

Many years after this volume was originally published, in the first of the series of poems titled "River," Harrison let us know, "I decided we were born to be moving water not ice."

THE THEORY &
PRACTICE OF RIVERS

THE THEORY & PRACTICE OF RIVERS

The rivers of my life:
moving looms of light,
anchored beneath the log
at night I can see the moon
up through the water
as shattered milk, the nudge
of fishes, belly and back
in turn grating against log
and bottom; and letting go, the current
lifts me up and out
into the dark, gathering motion,
drifting into an eddy
with a sideways swirl,
the sandbar cooler than the air:
to speak it clearly,
how the water goes
is how the earth is shaped.

It is not so much that I got
there from here, which is everyone's
story: but the shape
of the voyage, how it pushed
outward in every direction
until it stopped:
roots of plants and trees,
certain coral heads,
photos of splintered lightning,
blood vessels,
the shapes of creeks and rivers.

This is the ascent out of water:
there is no time but that
of convenience, time so that everything
won't happen at once; dark

doesn't fall—dark comes up
out of the earth, an exhalation.
It gathers itself close
to the ground, rising
to envelop us, as if the bottom
of the sea rose up to meet us.
Have you ever gone
to the bottom of the sea?

Mute unity of water.
I sculpted this girl
out of ice so beautifully
she was taken away.
How banal the swan song
which is a water song.
There never was a swan
who said goodbye. My raven
in the pine tree squawked his way
to death, falling from branch
to branch. To branch again.
To ground. The song, the muffle
of earth as the body falls,
feather against pine needles.

Near the estuary north of Guilford
my brother recites the Episcopalian
burial service over his dead daughter.
Gloria, as in *Gloria in Excelsis.*
I cannot bear this passion and courage;
my eyes turn toward the swamp
and sea, so blurred they'll never quite
clear themselves again. The inside of the eye,
vitreous humor, is the same pulp found
inside the squid. I can see Gloria
in the snow and in the water. She lives

in the snow and water and in my eyes.
This is a song for her.

Kokopele saved me this time:
flute song in soft dark
sound of water over rock,
the moon glitter rippling;
breath caught as my hunched
figure moved in a comic circle,
seven times around the cabin
through the woods in the dark.
Why did I decide to frighten myself?

Light snow in early May,
wolf prints in alluvial fan,
moving across the sandbar
in the river braided near its mouth
until the final twist; then the prints
move across drift ice in a dead
channel, and back into the swamp.

The closest I came to describing it:
it is early winter, mid-November
with light snow, the ground rock-hard
with frost. We are moving but I can't
seem to find my wife and two daughters.
I have left our old house and can't remember
how to find the new one.

The days are stacked against
what we think we are:
the story of the water babies
swimming up- and downstream
amid waterweed, twisting
with cherubic smiles in the current,
human and fish married.

Again! The girl I so painfully
sculpted out of ice
was taken away. She said:
"Goddamn the Lizard King,"
her night message and goodbye.
The days are stacked against
what we think we are:
near the raven rookery
inside the bend of river
with snowmelt and rain
flooding the bend; I've failed to stalk
these birds again and they flutter
and wheel above me with parental screams
saying, *Get out get out you bastard.*
The days are stacked against
what we think we are.
After a month of interior weeping
it occurred to me that in times like these
I have nothing to fall back on
except the sun and moon and earth.
I dress in camouflage and crawl
around swamps and forest, seeing
the bitch coyote five times but never
before she sees me. Her look
is curious, almost a smile.
The days are stacked against
what we think we are:
it is nearly impossible
to surprise ourselves
I will never wake up
and be able to play the piano.
South fifteen miles, still
near the river, calling coyotes
with Dennis E: full moon in east,

northern lights in pale green swirl,
from the west an immense line squall
and thunderstorm approaching off Lake Superior.
Failing with his call he uses
the song of the loon to bring
an answer from the coyotes.
"They can't resist it," he says.
The days are stacked against
what we think we are.
Standing in the river up to my waist
the infant beaver peeks at me
from the flooded tag alder
and approaches though warned
by her mother whacking her tail.
About seven feet away she bobs
to dive, mooning me with her small
pink ass, rising again for another
look, then downward swimming
past my leg, still looking.
The days are finally stacked
against what we think we are:
how long can I stare at the river?
Three months in a row now
with no signs of stopping,
glancing to the right, an almost
embarrassed feeling that the river
will stop flowing and I can go home.
The days, at last, are stacked against
what we think we are.
Who in their most hallowed, sleepless
night with the moon seven feet
outside the window, the moon
that the river swallows, would wish
it otherwise?

On New Year's Eve I'm wrapped
in my habits, looking up to the TV
to see the red ball, the apple,
rise or fall, I forget which:
a poem on the cherrywood table, a fire,
a blizzard, some whiskey, three
restless cats, and two sleeping dogs,
at home and making three gallons
of menudo for the revelers who'll
need it come tomorrow after amateur night:
about ten pounds of tripe, ancho,
molido, serrano, and chipotle pepper, cumin,
coriander, a few calves' or piglets' feet.
I don't wonder what is becoming
to the man already becoming.
I also added a half-quart of stock
left over from last night's bollito misto
wherein I poach for appropriate times:
fifteen pounds of veal bones to be discarded,
a beef brisket, a pork roast, Italian sausage,
a large barnyard hen, a pheasant, a guinea
hen, and for about thirty minutes until
rosy rare a whole filet, served with
three sauces: tomato coulis, piquante (anchovies & capers etc.)
and a rouille. Last week when my daughter
came home from NYC I made her venison
with truffles, also roast quail for Christmas
breakfast, also a wild turkey, some roast mallards & grouse,
also a cacciatore of rabbit & pheasant.
Oddly the best meal of the year
was in the cabin by the river:
a single fresh brook trout *au bleu*
with one boiled new potato and one
wild-leek vinaigrette. By the river

I try to keep alive, perhaps to write
more poems, though lately I think
of us all as lay-down comedians
who, when we finally tried to get up,
have found that our feet are mushy,
and what's more, no one cares
or bothers to read anymore those
sotto voce below-radar flights
from the empirical. But I am wrapped
in my habits. I must send my prayer
upward and downward. "Why do you write
poems?" the stewardess asked. "I guess
it's because every angel is terrible,
still though, alas, I invoke these almost
deadly birds of the soul,"
I cribbed from Rilke.

The travels on dry riverbeds: Salt River,
or nearly dry up Canyon de Chelly,
a half-foot of water—a skin over
the brown riverbed. The Navajo
family stuck with a load of dry
corn and crab apples. Only the woman
speaks English, the children at first shy
and frightened of my blind left eye
(some tribes attach importance to this—
strangely enough, this eye can see underwater).
We're up on the del Muerto fork and while
I'm kneeling in the water shoving rocks
under the axle I glance skyward
at an Anasazi cliff dwelling, the "ancient
ones" they're called. This morning
a young schizophrenic Navajo attacked
our truck with a club, his head seeming
to turn nearly all the way around as

an owl's. Finally the children smile
as the truck is pulled free. I am given
a hatful of the most delicious crab apples
in the world. I watch the first apple
core float west on the slender current,
my throat a knot of everything
I no longer understand.

Sitting on the bank, the water
stares back so deeply you can hear
it afterward when you wish. It is the water
of dreams, and for the nightwalker
who can almost walk on the water,
it is most of all the water of awakening,
passing with the speed of life
herself, drifting in circles in an eddy
joining the current again
as if the eddy were a few moments' sleep.

The story can't hesitate to stop.
I can't find a river in Los Angeles
except the cement one behind Sportsman's Lodge
on Ventura. There I feel my
high blood pressure like an electric tiara
around my head, a small comic cloud,
a miniature junkyard where my confused
desires, hopes, hates, and loves short circuit
in little puffs of hissing ozone. And the women
are hard green horses disappearing,
concealing themselves in buildings and tops
of wild palms in ambush.
A riverless city of redolent
and banal sobs, green girls
in trees, girls hard as basalt.
"My grandfather screwed me

when I was seven years old,"
she said, while I looked out
at the cement river flowing with dusty rain,
at three dogs playing in the cement river.
"He's dead now so there's no point
sweating it," she added.

Up in the Amazon River Basin
during a dark time Matthiessen built
a raft with a native, chewed some coca leaves,
boarded the raft and off they went on a river
not on any map, uncharted, wanting to see
the Great Mother of Snakes; a truncated
version of our voyage of seventy years—
actuarial average. To see green and live green,
moving on water sometimes clouded often clear.
Now our own pond is white with ice.
In the barnyard lying in the snow
I can hear the underground creek,
a creek without a name.

I forgot to tell you that while
I was away my heart broke
and I became not so much old, but older,
definably older within a few days.
This happened on a cold dawn in New Iberia
while I was feeding a frightened stray
dog a sack of pork rinds in the rain.

Three girls danced the Cotton-Eyed Joe,
almost sedate, erect, with relentless grace,
where did they come from
and where did they go
in ever-so-delicate circles?
And because of time, circles

that no longer close
or return to themselves.

I rode the gray horse
all day in the rain.
The fields became unmoving rivers,
the trees foreshortened.
I saw a girl in a white dress
standing half-hidden in the water
behind a maple tree.
I pretended not to notice
and made a long slow circle
behind a floating hedgetop
to catch her unawares.
She was gone but I had that prickly
fear someone was watching from a tree,
far up in a leaf-veil of green maple leaves.
Now the horse began swimming
toward higher ground, from where
I watched the tree until dark.

"Life, this vastly mysterious process
to which our culture inures us
lest we become useless citizens!
And is it terrible to be lonely and ill?"
she wrote. "Not at all, in fact, it is better
to be lonely when ill. To others, friends,
relatives, loved ones, death is our most
interesting, our most dramatic act.
Perhaps the best thing I've learned
from these apparently cursed and bedraggled
Indians I've studied all these years
is how to die. Last year I sat beside
a seven-year-old Hopi girl as she sang
her death song in a slight quavering

voice. Who among us whites, child
or adult, will sing while we die?"

On Whitefish Bay, the motor broke down
in heavy seas. We chopped ice off the gunwales
quite happily as it was unlikely we'd survive
and it was something to do. Ted just sat there
out of the wind and spray, drinking whiskey.
"I been on the wagon for a year. If I'm going
to die by god at least I get to have a drink."

What is it to actually go outside the nest
we have built for ourselves, and earlier
our father's nest: to go into a forest
alone with our eyes open? It's different
when you don't know what's over the hill—
keep the river on your left, then you see
the river on your right. I have simply
forgotten left and right, even up and down,
whirl then sleep on a cloudy day to forget
direction. It is hard to learn how
to be lost after so much training.

In New York I clocked
seven tugboats on the East River
in less than a half hour;
then I went to a party
where very rich people
talked about their arches,
foot arches, not architectural arches.
Back at my post I dozed
and saw only one more tugboat
before I slept.

But in New York I also saw a big hole
of maddened pipes with all the direction

of the swastika and a few immigrants
figuring it all out with the impenetrable
good sense of those who do the actual
work of the world.

How did I forget that rich turbulent
river, so cold in the rumply brown folds
of spring; by August cool, clear, glittery
in the sunlight; umbrous as it dips
under the logjam. In May, the river
a roar beyond a thin wall of sleep, with
the world of snow still gliding in rivulets
down imperceptible slopes; in August
through the screened window against which
bugs and moths scratch so lightly,
as lightly as the river sounds.

How can I renew oaths
I can't quite remember?
In New Orleans I was light in body and soul
because of food poisoning, the bathroom gymnastics
of flesh against marble floor,
seeing the underside of the bathtub
for the first time since I was a child,
and the next day crossing Cajun bridges
in the Atchafalaya, where Blacks were thrown
to alligators I'm told, Black souls whirling
in brown water, whirling
in an immaculate crawfish
rosary.

In the water I can remember
women I didn't know: Adriana
dancing her way home at the end
of a rope, a cool Tuscany night,
the apple tree in bloom;

the moon which I checked
was not quite full, a half-moon,
the rest of the life abandoned to the dark.

I warned myself all night
but then halfway between my ears
I turned toward the heavens
and reached the top of my head.
From there I can go just about
anywhere I want and I've never
found my way back home.

This isn't the old song
of the suicidal house,
I forgot the tune about small
windows growing smaller, the door
neither big enough to enter
nor exit, the sinking hydraulic ceilings
and the attic full of wet cement.
I wanted to go to the Camargue,
to Corsica, to return to Costa Rica,
but I couldn't escape the suicidal house
until May when I drove
through the snow to reach the river.

On the bank by the spring creek
my shadow seemed to leap
up to gather me, or it leapt
up to gather me, not seeming so
but as a natural fact. Faulkner said
that the drowned man's shadow had watched
him from the river all the time.

Drowning in the bourgeois trough,
a *bourride* or gruel of money, drugs,
whiskey, hotels, the dream coasts,

ass in the air at the trough, drowning
in a river of pus, pus of civilization,
pus of cities, unholy river of shit,
of filth, shit of nightmares, shit
of skewed dreams and swallowed years.
The river pulls me out,
draws me elsewhere
and down to blue water,
green water,
black water.

How far between the Virgin
and the Garrison and back?
Why is it a hundred times farther to get back,
the return upriver in the dark?
It isn't innocence, but to win back breath,
body heat, the light that gathers around
a waking animal. Ten years ago I saw
the dancing Virgin in a basement
in New York, a whirl of hot color
from floor to ceiling, whirling in a dance.
At eighteen in New York
on Grove Street I discovered
red wine, garlic, Rimbaud,
and a red-haired girl. Livid colors
not known in farm country,
also Charlie Parker, Sonny Rollins,
the odors from restaurant vents,
thirty-five-cent Italian sausages
on MacDougal, and the Hudson River:
days of river-watching and trying
to get on a boat for the tropics and see
that Great Ocean river, the Gulf Stream.
Another fifteen years before I saw
the Ocean river and the sharks hanging

under the sargassum weed lines,
a blue river in green water,
and the sharks staring back, sinking
down listlessly into darker water;
the torpor of heat, a hundred low-tide
nights begging a forgetfulness
I haven't quite earned.

I forgot where I heard that poems
are designed to waken sleeping gods;
in our time they've taken on nearly
unrecognizable shapes as gods will do;
one is a dog, one is a scarecrow
that doesn't work—crows perch
on the wind-whipped sleeves,
one is a carpenter who doesn't become Jesus,
one is a girl who went to heaven
sixty years early. Gods die,
and not always out of choice,
like nearsighted cats jumping
between buildings seven stories up.
One god drew feathers out of my skin
so I could fly, a favor close to terror.
But this isn't a map of the gods.
When they live in rivers
it's because rivers have no equilibrium;
gods resent equilibrium when everything
that lives *moves;* boulders
are a war of atoms, and the dandelion
cracks upward through the blacktop road.
Seltzer's tropical beetle grew
from a larval lump in a man's arm,
emerging full grown, pincers waving.
On Mt. Cuchama there were so many
gods passing through I hid in a hole

in a rock, waking one by accident.
I fled with a tight ass and cold skin.
I could draw a map of this place
but they're never caught in the same location
twice. And their voices change from involuntary
screams to the singular wail of the loon,
possibly the wind that can howl down Wall St.
Gods have long abandoned the banality of war
though they were stirred by a hundred-year-old
guitarist I heard in Brazil, also the autistic child
at the piano. We'll be greeted at death
so why should I wait? Today I invoked
any available god back in the woods in the fog.
The world was white with last week's melting
blizzard, the fog drifting upward, then descending.
The only sound was a porcupine eating bark
off an old tree, and a rivulet beneath the snow.
Sometimes the obvious is true: the full
moon on her bare bottom by the river!
For the gay, the full moon on the lover's prick!
Gods laugh at the fiction of gender.
Water-gods, moon-gods, god-fever,
sun-gods, fire-gods, give this earth-diver
more songs before I die.

A "system" suggests the cutting off,
i.e., in channel morphology, the reduction,
the suppression of texture to simplify:
to understand a man, or woman, growing
old with eagerness you first consider
the sensuality of death, an unacknowledged
surprise to most. In nature the physiology
has heat and color, beast and tree
saying aloud the wonder of death;

to study rivers, including the postcard
waterfalls, is to adopt another life;
a limited life attaches itself to the endless
movement, the renowned underground
rivers of South America which I've felt
thundering far beneath my feet—to die
is to descend into such rivers and flow
along in the perfect dark. But aboveground
I'm memorizing life, from the winter moon
to the sound of my exhaustion in March
when all the sodden plans have collapsed
and only daughters, the dogs and cats
keep one from disappearing at gunpoint.
I brought myself here and stare nose to nose
at the tolerant cat who laps whiskey
from my mustache. Life often shatters
in schizoid splinters. I will avoid
becoming the cold stone wall I am straddling.

I had forgot what it was I liked
about life. I hear if you own a chimpanzee
they cease at a point to be funny. Writers
and politicians share an embarrassed moment
when they are sure all problems will disappear
if you get the language right.
That's not all they share—in each other's
company they are like boys who have been
discovered at wiener-play in the toilet.
At worst, it's the gift of gab.
At best it's Martin Luther King and Rimbaud.
Bearing down hard on love and death
there is an equal and opposite reaction.
All these years they have split the pie,
leaving the topping for the preachers

who don't want folks to fuck or eat.
What kind of magic, or rite of fertility,
to transcend this shit-soaked stew?

The river is as far as I can move
from the world of numbers: I'm all
for full retreats, escapes, a 47 yr. old runaway.
"Gettin' too old to run away," I wrote
but not quite believing this option is gray.
I stare into the deepest pool of the river
which holds the mystery of a cellar to a child,
and think of those two-track roads that dwindle
into nothing in the forest. I have this feeling
of walking around for days with the wind
knocked out of me. In the cellar was a root
cellar where we stored potatoes, apples, carrots
and where a family of harmless blacksnakes lived.
In certain rivers there are pools a hundred
foot deep. In a swamp I must keep secret
there is a deep boiling spring around which
in the dog days of August large brook trout
swim and feed. An adult can speak dreams
to children saying that there is a spring
that goes down to the center of the earth.
Maybe there is. Next summer I'm designing
and building a small river about seventy-seven
foot long. It will flow both ways, in reverse
of nature. I will build a dam and blow it up.

The involuntary image that sweeps
into the mind, irresistible and without evident
cause as a dream or thunderstorm,
or rising to the surface from childhood,
the longest journey taken in a split second,
from there to now, without pause:

in the woods with Mary Cooper, my first love
wearing a violet scarf in May. We're
looking after her huge mongoloid aunt,
trailing after this woman who loves us
but so dimly perceives the world. We pick
and clean wild leeks for her. The creek
is wild and dangerous with the last
of the snowmelt. The child-woman
tries to enter the creek and we tackle her.
She's stronger, then slowly understands,
half-wet and muddy. She kisses me
while Mary laughs, then Mary kisses me
over and over. Now I see the pools
in the mongol eyes that watch and smile
with delight and hear the roar of the creek,
smell the scent of leeks on her muddy lips.

This is an obscene koan set plumb
in the middle of the Occident:
the man with three hands lacks symmetry
but claps the loudest, the chicken
in circles on the sideless road, a plane
that takes off and can never land.
I am not quite alert enough to live.
The fallen nest and fire in the closet,
my world without guardrails, the electric
noose, the puddle that had no bottom.
The fish in underground rivers are white
and blind as the porpoises who live far up
the muddy Amazon. In New York and LA
you don't want to see, hear, smell,
and you only open your mouth in restaurants.
At night you touch people with rock-hard skins.
I'm trying to become alert enough to live.
Yesterday after the blizzard I hiked far back

in a new swamp and found an iceless
pond connected to the river by a small creek.
Against deep white snow and black trees
there was a sulfurous fumarole, rank and sharp
in cold air. The water bubbled up brown,
then spread in turquoise to deep black,
without the track of a single mammal to drink.
This was nature's own, a beauty too strong
for life; a place to drown not live.

On waking after the accident
I was presented with the "whole picture"
as they say, magnificently detailed,
a child's diorama of what life appears to be:
staring at the picture I became drowsy
with relief when I noticed a yellow
dot of light in the lower right-hand corner.
I unhooked the machines and tubes and crawled
to the picture, with an eyeball to the dot
of light, which turned out to be a miniature
tunnel at the end of which I could see
mountains and stars whirling and tumbling,
sheets of emotions, vertical rivers, upside-
down lakes, herds of unknown mammals, birds
shedding feathers and regrowing them instantly,
snakes with feathered heads eating their own
shed skins, fish swimming straight up,
the bottom of Isaiah's robe, live whales
on dry ground, lions drinking from a golden
bowl of milk, the rush of night,
and somewhere in this the murmur of gods—
a tree-rubbing-tree music, a sweet howl
of water and rock-grating-rock, fire
hissing from fissures, the moon settled
comfortably on the ground, beginning to roll.

KOBUN

Hotei didn't need a *zafu,*
saying that his ass was sufficient.
The head's a cloud anchor
that the feet must follow.
Travel light, he said,
or don't travel at all.

LOOKING FORWARD TO AGE

I will walk down to a marina
on a hot day and not go out to sea.

I will go to bed and get up early,
and carry too much cash in my wallet.

On Memorial Day I will visit the graves
of all those who died in my novels.

If I have become famous I'll wear a green
janitor's suit and row a wooden boat.

From a key ring on my belt will hang
thirty-three keys that open no doors.

Perhaps I'll take all of my grandchildren
to Disneyland in a camper but probably not.

One day standing in a river with my fly rod
I'll have the courage to admit my life.

In a one-room cabin at night I'll consign
photos, all tentative memories to the fire.

And you my loves, few as there have been, let's lie
and say it could never have been otherwise.

So that: we may glide off in peace, not howling
like orphans in this endless century of war.

HOMILY

These simple rules to live within—a black
pen at night, a gold pen in daylight,
avoid blue food and ten-ounce shots
of whiskey, don't point a gun at yourself,
don't snipe with the cri-cri-cri of a *becassine,*
don't use gas for starter fluid, don't read
dirty magazines in front of stewardesses—
it happens all the time; it's time to stop
cleaning your plate, forget the birthdays
of the dead, give all you can to the poor.
This might go on and on and will: who can
choose between the animal in the road
and the ditch? A magnum for lunch
is a little too much but not enough
for dinner. Polish the actual stars at night
as an invisible man pets a dog, an actual
man a memory-dog lost under
the morning glory trellis forty years ago.
Dance with yourself with all your heart
and soul, and occasionally others, but don't
eat all the berries birds eat or you'll die.
Kiss yourself in the mirror but don't fall in love
with photos of ladies in magazines. Don't fall
in love as if you were falling through
the floor in an abandoned house, or off
a dock at night, or down a crevasse
covered with false snow, a cow floundering
in quicksand while the other cows watch
without particular interest, backward
off a crumbling cornice. Don't fall in love
with two at once. From the ceiling you can see
this circle of three, though one might be elsewhere.

He is rended, he rends himself, he dances,
he whirls so hard everything he *is* flies off.
He crumples as paper but rises daily from the dead.

SOUTHERN CROSS

That hot desert beach in Ecuador,
with scarcely a splotch of vegetation
fronting as it does
a Pacific so immensely lush
it hurls lobsters on great flat
boulders where children brave fatal
waves to pick them up.
Turning from one to the other quickly,
it is incomprehensible: from wild, gray
sunblasted burro eating cactus to azure
immensity of ocean, from miniature
goat dead on infantile feet in sand
to imponderable roar of swells, equatorial sun;
music that squeezes the blood out of the heart
by midnight, and girls whose legs
glisten with sweat, their teeth white
as Canadian snow, legs pounding as plump
brown pistons, and night noises I've
never heard, though at the coolest period
in these latitudes, near the faintest
beginning of dawn, there was the cold
unmistakable machine gun, the harshest
chatter death can make. Only then do
I think of my very distant relative, Lorca,
that precocious skeleton, as he crumpled
earthward against brown pine needles;
and the sky, vaster than the Pacific,
whirled overhead, a sky without birds or clouds,
azul te quiero azul.

SULLIVAN POEM

March 5: first day without a fire.
Too early. Too early. Too early!
Take joy in the day
without consideration, the three
newly-brought-to-life bugs
who are not meant to know
what they are doing avoid each other
on windows stained
by a dozen storms.

We eat our father's food:
herring, beans, salt pork,
sauerkraut, pig hocks, salt cod.
I have said goodbye with one thousand
laments so that even the heart of the rose
becomes empty as my dog's rubber ball.
The dead are not meant to go,
but to trail off so that one can
see them on a distant hillock,
across the river, in dreams
from which one awakens nearly healed:
don't worry, it's fine to be dead,
they say; we were a little early
but could not help ourselves.
Everyone dies as the child they were,
and at the moment, this secret,
intricately concealed heart blooms
forth with the first song anyone
sang in the dark, "Now I lay me
down to sleep, I pray the Lord
my soul to keep . . ."

Now this oddly gentle winter, almost dulcet,
winds to a blurred close with trees full
of birds that belong farther south,
and people are missing something
to complain about; a violent March
is an unacknowledged prayer;
a rape of nature, a healing blizzard,
a very near disaster.

So this last lament:
as unknowable as the eye of the crow
staring down from the walnut tree,
blind as the Magellanic clouds,
as cold as that March mud puddle
at the foot of the granary steps,
unseeable as the birthright of the LA
whore's Nebraska childhood of lilacs
and cornfields and an unnamed prairie
bird that lived in a thicket
where she hid,
as treacherous as a pond's spring
ice to a child,
black as the scar of a half-peeled
birch tree,
the wrench of the beast's heart just
short of the waterhole,
as bell-clear as a gunshot at dawn,
is the ache of a father's death.

It is that, but far more:
as if we take a voyage out of life
as surely as we took a voyage in,
almost as frightened children

in a cellar's cold gray air;
or before memory—they put me on a boat
on this river, then I was lifted off;
in our hearts, it is always just after
dawn, and each bird's song is the first,
and that ever-so-slight breeze that touches
the tops of trees and ripples the lake
moves through our bodies as if we were gods.

HORSE

What if it were our privilege
to sculpt our dreams of animals?
But those shapes in the night
come and go too quickly to be held
in stone: but not to avoid these shapes
as if dreams were only a nighttime
pocket to be remembered and avoided.
Who can say in the depths of
his life and heart what beast
most stopped life, the animals
he watched, the animals he only touched
in dreams? Even our hearts don't beat
the way we want them to. What
can we know in that waking,
sleeping edge? We put down
my daughter's old horse, old and
arthritic, a home burial. By dawn with eye
half-open, I said to myself, is
he still running, is he still running
around, under the ground?

COBRA

What are these nightmares,
so wildly colored? We're in every
movie we see, even in our sleep.
Not that we can become what
we fear most but that we can't
resist ourselves. The grizzly
attack; after that divorce
and standing outside the school
with a rifle so they can't take my
daughter Anna. By god! Long ago
in Kenya where I examined the
grass closely before I sat down
to a poisonous lunch, I worried
about cobras. When going insane I worried
about cobra venom in Major Grey's Chutney.
Simple as that. Then in overnight sleep I became
a lordly cobra, feeling the pasture grass
at high noon glide beneath my
stomach. I watched the house with
my head arched above the weeds,
then slept in the cool dirt under the granary.

PORPOISE

Every year, when we're fly-fishing for tarpon
off Key West, Guy insists that porpoises
are good luck. But it's not so banal
as catching more fish or having a fashion
model fall out of the sky lightly on your head,
or at your feet depending on certain
preferences. It's what porpoises do to the ocean.
You see a school making love off Boca Grande,
the baby with his question mark staring
at us a few feet from the boat.
Porpoises dance for as long as they live.
You can do nothing for them.
They alter the universe.

THE BRAND NEW STATUE OF LIBERTY

to Lee Iacocca (another Michigan boy)

I was commissioned in a dream by Imanja,
also the Black Pope of Brazil, Tancred,
to design a seven-tiered necklace
of seven thousand skulls for the Statue of Liberty.
Of course from a distance they'll look
like pearls, but in November
when the strongest winds blow, the skulls
will rattle wildly, bone against metal,
a crack and chatter of bone against metal,
the true sound of history, this metal striking bone.
I'm not going to get heavy-handed—
a job is a job and I've leased a football
field for the summer, gathered a group of ladies
who are art lovers, leased in advance
a bull Sikorsky freight helicopter
to drop on the necklace: funding comes
from Ford Foundation, Rockefeller, the NEA.
There is one Jewish skull from Atlanta, two
from Mississippi, but this is basically
an indigenous cast except skulls from tribes
of Blacks who got a free ride over from Africa,
representative skulls from all the Indian
tribes, an assortment of grizzly, wolf,
coyote and buffalo skulls. But what beauty
when the morning summer sun glances
off these bony pates! And her great
iron lips quivering in a smile, almost a smirk
so that she'll drop the torch to fondle the jewels.

THE TIMES ATLAS

For my mentor, long dead, Richard Halliburton
and his Seven League Boots

Today was the coldest day in the history
of the Midwest. Thank god for the moon
in this terrible storm.

There are areas far out at sea where
it rains a great deal. Camus said
it rained so hard even the sea was wet.

O god all our continents are only rifted
magma welled up from below. We don't
have a solid place to stand.

A little bullshit here as the Nile
is purportedly eighty miles longer
than the Amazon. I proclaim it a tie.

Pay out your 125 bucks and find out the world
isn't what you think it is but what
it is. We whirl so nothing falls off.
Eels, polar bears, bugs and men enjoy

the maker's design. No one really
leaves this place. O loveliness
of Caribbean sun off water under
trade wind's lilt.

Meanwhile the weather is no longer amusing.
Earth frightens me, the blizzard, house's
shudder, oceanic roar, the brittle night
that might leave so many dead.

NEW LOVE

With these dire portents
we'll learn the language
of knees, shoulder blades,
chins but not the first floor up,
shinbones, the incomprehensible
belly buttons of childhood,
heels and the soles of our feet,
spines and neckbones,
risqué photos of the tender
inside of elbows, tumescent fingers
draw the outlines of lost parts
on the wall; bottom and pubis
Delphic, unapproachable as Jupiter,
a memory worn as the first love
we knew, ourselves a test pattern
become obsession: this love
in the plague years—we used to kiss
a mirror to see if we were dead.
Now we relearn the future as we learned
to walk, as a baby grabs its toes,
tilts backward, rocking. Tonight I'll touch
your wrist and in a year perhaps grind
my blind eye's socket against your hipbone.
With all this death, behind our backs,
the moon has become the moon again.

WHAT HE SAID WHEN I WAS ELEVEN

August, a dense heat wave at the cabin
mixed with torrents of rain,
the two-tracks become miniature rivers.

In the Russian Orthodox Church
one does not talk to God, one sings.
This empty and sunblasted land

has a voice rising in shimmers.
I did not sing in Moscow
but St. Basil's in Leningrad raised

a quiet tune. But now seven worlds
away I hang the *cazas-moscas*
from the ceiling and catch seven flies

in the first hour, buzzing madly
against the stickiness. I've never seen
the scissor-tailed flycatcher, a favorite

bird of my youth, the worn Audubon
card pinned to the wall. When I miss
flies three times with the swatter

they go free for good. Fair is fair.
There is too much nature pressing against
the window as if it were a green night;

and the river swirling in glazed turbulence
is less friendly than ever before.
Forty years ago she called, *Come home, come home,*

it's suppertime. I was fishing a fishless
cattle pond with a new three-dollar pole,
dreaming the dark blue ocean of pictures.

In the barn I threw down hay
while my Swede grandpa finished milking,
squirting the barn cat's mouth with an udder.

I kissed the wet nose of my favorite cow,
drank a dipper of fresh warm milk
and carried two pails to the house,

scraping the manure off my feet
in the pump shed. She poured the milk
in the cream separator and I began cranking.

At supper the oilcloth was decorated
with worn pink roses. We ate cold herring,
also the bluegills we had caught at daylight.

The fly-strip above the table idled in
the window's breeze, a new fly in its death buzz.
Grandpa said, "We are all flies."

That's what he said forty years ago.

ACTING

for J.N.

In the best sense,
becoming another
so that there is no trace left
of what we think is the self.
I am whoever.
It is not gesture
but the cortex of gesture,
not movement
but the soul of movement.
Look at the earth with your left eye
and at the sky with your right.
Worship contraries.
What makes us alike
is also what makes us different.
From Man to Jokester to Trickster
is a nudge toward the deep,
the incalculable abyss
you stare into so it will
stare back into you.
We are our consciousness
and it is the god in us
who struggles to be in everyone
in order to be ourselves.
When you see the chalked form
of the murdered man on the cement
throw yourself onto it and feel
the heat of the stone-hard fit.
This is the liquid poem,
the forefinger traced around both
the neck and the sun:
to be and be and be

as a creek turns corners
by grace of volume, heft of water,
speed by rate of drop,
even the contour of stone
changing day by day.
So that: when you wake in the night,
the freedom of the nightmare
turned to dream follows you
into morning, and there is no
skin on earth you cannot enter,
no beast or plant,
no man or woman
you may not flow through
and become.

MY FRIEND THE BEAR

Down in the bone myth of the cellar
of this farmhouse, behind the empty fruit jars
the whole wall swings open to the room
where I keep the bear. There's a tunnel
to the outside on the far wall that emerges
in the lilac grove in the backyard
but she rarely uses it, knowing there's no room
around here for a freewheeling bear.
She's not a dainty eater so once a day
I shovel shit while she lopes in playful circles.
Privately she likes religion—from the bedroom
I hear her incantatory moans and howls
below me—and April 23rd, when I open
the car trunk and whistle at midnight
and she shoots up the tunnel, almost airborne
when she meets the night. We head north
and her growls are less friendly as she scents
the forest-above-the-road smell. I release
her where I found her as an orphan three
years ago, bawling against the dead carcass
of her mother. I let her go at the head
of the gully leading down to the swamp,
jumping free of her snarls and roars.
But each October 9th, one day before bear season
she reappears at the cabin frightening
the bird dogs. We embrace ear to ear,
her huge head on my shoulder,
her breathing like god's.

CABIN POEM

I

The blond girl
with a polka heart:
one foot, then another,
then aerial
in a twisting jump,
chin upward
with a scream of such
splendor
I go back to my cabin,
and start a fire.

II

Art & life
drunk & sober
empty & full
guilt & grace
cabin & home
north & south
struggle & peace
after which we catch
a glimpse of stars,
the white glistening pelt
of the Milky Way,
hear the startled bear crashing
through the delta swamp below me.
In these troubled times
I go inside and start a fire.

III

I am the bird that hears the worm,
or, my cousin said, the pulse of a wound
that probes to the opposite side.
I have abandoned alcohol, cocaine,
the news, and outdoor prayer
as support systems.
How can you make a case for yourself
before an ocean of trees, or standing
waist-deep in the river? Or sitting
on the logjam with a pistol?
I reject oneness with bears.
She has two cubs and thinks she
owns the swamp I thought I bought.
I shoot once in the air to tell her
it's my turn at the logjam
for an hour's thought about nothing.
Perhaps that is oneness with bears.
I've decided to make up my mind
about nothing, to assume the water mask,
to finish my life disguised as a creek,
an eddy, joining at night the full,
sweet flow, to absorb the sky,
to swallow the heat and cold, the moon
and the stars, to swallow myself
in ceaseless flow.

RICH FOLKS, POOR FOLKS, AND NEITHER

I

Rich folks keep their teeth
until late in life,
and park their cars in heated garages.
They own kitsch statues of praying hands
that conceal seven pounds of solid gold,
knowing that burglars hedge at icons.
At the merest twinge they go to the dentist,
and their dogs' anuses are professionally
inspected for unsuspected diseases.
Rich folks dream of the perfect massage
that will bring secret, effortless orgasm,
and absolutely super and undiscovered
islands with first-rate hotels
where they will learn to windsurf
in five minutes. They buy clothes that fit—
a forty waist means forty pants—rich folks
don't squeeze into thirty-eights. At spas
they are not too critical of their big asses,
and they believe in real small portions
because they can eat again pretty quick.
Rich folks resent richer folks
and they also resent poor folks
for their failures at meniality.
It's unfortunate for our theory that the same
proportion of rich folks are as pleasant
as poor folks, a pitiless seven
percent, though not necessarily the ones
who still say their prayers and finish
the morning oatmeal to help the poor.
Everyone I have ever met is deeply
puzzled.

II

Up in Michigan poor folks dream of trips
to Hawaii or "Vegas." They muttered deeply
when the banker won the big lottery—
"It just don't seem fair," they said.
Long ago when I was poor
there was something in me that craved
to get fired, to drink a shot and beer
with a lump in my throat, hitchhike
or drive to California in an old car,
tell my family "I'll write if I get work."
In California, where you can sleep outside
every night, I saw the Pacific Ocean
and ate my first food of the Orient,
a fifty-cent bowl of noodles and pork.
No more cornmeal mush with salt pork
gravy, no more shovels at dawn,
no more clothes smelling of kerosene,
no more girls wearing ankle bracelets spelling
another's name. No more three-hour waits
in unemployment lines, or cafeteria catsup
and bread for fifteen cents. I've eaten
my last White Tower burger and I'm heading
for the top. Or not. How could I dream
I'd end up moist-eyed in the Beverly Hills Hotel
when I ordered thirteen appetizers for myself
and the wheels of the laden trolley squeaked?
The television in the limousine broke down
and I missed the news on the way to look
at the ocean where there were no waves.
When I went bankrupt I began to notice cemeteries
and wore out my clothes, drank up the wine cellar.

I went to the movies and kissed my wife a lot
for the same reason—they're both in technicolor.
Everyone I met in those days was deeply puzzled.

III

Now I've rubbed rich and poor together
like two grating stones, mixed them temporarily
like oil and vinegar, male and female, until
my interest has waned to nothing. One night I saw
a constellation that chose not to reappear,
drifting in the day into another galaxy.
I tried to ignore the sound of my footsteps
in the woods until I did, and when I swam
in the river I finally forgot it was water,
but I still can't see a cow without saying *cow.*
Perhaps this was not meant to be. I dug
a deep hole out in a clearing in the forest
and sat down in it, studying the map
of the sky above me for clues, a new bible.
This is rushing things a bit, I thought.
I became a woman then became a man again.
I hiked during the night alone and gave
my dogs fresh bones until they no longer cared.
I bought drinks for the poor and for myself,
left mail unopened, didn't speak on the phone,
only listened. I shot the copy machine with my rifle.
No more copies, I thought, everything original!
Now I am trying to unlearn the universe
in the usual increments of nights and days.
Time herself often visits in swirling but gentle clouds.
Way out there on the borders of my consciousness
I've caught glimpses of that great dark bird,
the beating of whose wings is death, drawing closer.
How could it be otherwise? I thought.

Down in the hole last August during a thunderstorm
I watched her left wingtip shudder past
between two lightning strokes. Maybe I'll see her again
during the northern lights, but then, at that moment,
I was still a child of water and mud.

DANCING

After the passing of irresistible
music you must learn to make
do with a dripping faucet,
rain or sleet on the roof,
eventually snow,
a cat's sigh,
the spherical notes that float
down from Aldebaran,
your cells as they part,
craving oxygen.

THE IDEA OF BALANCE IS TO BE FOUND
IN HERONS AND LOONS

I just heard a loon-call on a TV ad
and my body gave itself
a quite voluntary shudder,
as in the night in East Africa
I heard the immense barking cough
of a lion, so foreign and indifferent.

But the lion drifts away
and the loon stays close,
calling, as she did in my childhood,
in the cold rain a song
that tells the world of men
to keep its distance.

It isn't the signal of another life
or the reminder of anything
except her call: still,
at this quiet point past midnight
the rain is the same rain
that fell so long ago, and the loon
says I'm seven years old again.

At the far ends of the lake
where no one lives or visits—
there are no roads to get there;
you take the watercourse way,
the quiet drip and drizzle
of oars, slight squeak of oarlock,
the bare feet can feel the cold water
move beneath the old wood boat.

At one end the lordly great blue herons
nest at the top of the white pine;
at the other end the loons,
just after daylight in cream-colored mist,
drifting with wails that begin as querulous,
rising then into the spheres in volume,
with lost or doomed angels imprisoned
within their breasts.

SMALL POEM

There's something I've never known
when I get up in the morning.
Dead children fly off in the shape
of question marks, the doe's backward
glance at the stillborn fawn.
I don't know what it is
in the morning, as if incomprehension
beds down with me on waking.
What is the precise emotional temperature
when the young man hangs himself
in the jail cell with his father's belt?
What is the foot size of the Beast of Belsen?
This man in his overremembered life
needs to know the source of the ache
which is an answer without a question,
his fingers wrapped around the memory
of life, as Cleopatra's around the snake's neck,
a shepherd's crook of love.

COUNTING BIRDS

for Gerald Vizenor

As a child, fresh out of the hospital
with tape covering the left side
of my face, I began to count birds.
At age fifty the sum total is precise
and astonishing, my only secret.
Some men count women or the cars
they've owned, their shirts—
long sleeved and short sleeved—
or shoes, but I have my birds,
excluding, of course, those extraordinary
days: the twenty-one thousand
snow geese and sandhill cranes at
Bosque del Apache; the sky blinded
by great frigate birds in the Pacific
off Anconcito, Ecuador; the twenty-one
thousand pink flamingos in Ngorongoro Crater
in Tanzania; the vast flock of seabirds
on the Seri coast of the Sea of Cortez
down in Sonora that left at nightfall,
then reappeared, resuming
their exact positions at dawn;
the one thousand cliff swallows nesting
in the sand cliffs of Pyramid Point,
their small round burrows like eyes,
really the souls of the Anasazi who flew
here a thousand years ago
to wait the coming of the Manitou.
And then there were the usual, almost deadly
birds of the soul—the crow with silver
harness I rode one night as if she
were a black, feathered angel;

the birds I became to escape unfortunate
circumstances—how the skin ached
as the feathers shot out toward light;
the thousand birds the dogs helped
me shoot to become a bird (grouse, woodcock,
duck, dove, snipe, pheasant, prairie chicken, etc.).
On my deathbed I'll write this secret
number on a slip of paper and pass
it to my wife and two daughters.
It will be a hot evening in late June
and they might be glancing out the window
at the thunderstorm's approach from the west.
Looking past their eyes and a dead fly
on the window screen I'll wonder
if there's a bird waiting for me in the onrushing clouds.
O birds, I'll sing to myself, *you've carried*
me along on this bloody voyage,
carry me now into that cloud,
into the marvel of this final night.

HANDWRITTEN DRAFT OF
"THE THEORY & PRACTICE
OF RIVERS"

EDITOR'S NOTE

Jim Harrison wrote by hand, on yellow legal pads or in his notebooks, using a fine-point black pen. Whether writing fiction, nonfiction, or poetry, his creative process would not tolerate a keyboard or lighted screen between him and his words. For Jim, writing was intimate handwork.

In *Braided Creek: A Conversation in Poetry,* he writes:

> The Pilot razor-point pen is my
> compass, watch, and soul chaser.
> Thousands of miles of black squiggles.

Reading this handwritten draft of "The Theory & Practice of Rivers" is to travel upstream toward the source. Along the right-hand border of page one we see a list of nearly three dozen rivers below the heading "A few I have fished, swum, walked, hunted beside." Throughout the pages we also see word changes, strike outs, directional arrows, shifts in handwriting, and notes to self, though mostly we witness a grief-inspired poet in a surging creative groove, composing lines and stanzas and page after page that remained unchanged from first draft to final publication. In this era when most creative writing is composed and refined with the aid of electronic tools, this old-school holograph is a marvel to behold. And inspired by Rebecca Solnit's introduction to this volume, let's imagine that the liquid flowing out of Jim's pen over the decades, those "thousands of miles of black squiggles," were creeks and streams and rivers, and Jim Harrison was the headwaters.

Our thanks to Jim's daughters and the James T. Harrison Trust for their gracious permission to share this archival material. And deep bows of gratitude to the dedicated archivists at Grand Valley State University in Allendale, Michigan, where Jim Harrison's exhaustive literary archive is housed and awaiting your visit.

Joseph Bednarik
near Chimacum Creek

a few I have
fished, some
walked, heard
beside

the rivers of my life:
moving looms full of light,
anchored beneath the log
at night I can see the moon up through water
as shattered milk, the nudge
of fishes, belly and back
in turn grating against log
and bottom; and letting go, the current
sweeps lifts me up and out
into the night out, gathering motion,
then drifting into an eddy
with a sideways swirl, the
sandbar cooler than the air.

X   to speak it clearly shaped
     how the earth is shaped
     is now its water goes

It is not so much that I got
there from here, which is everyone's
story: but that the shape
of the voyage, how it pushed
outward in every direction
until it stopped:
            roots of plants and trees,
            certain coral heads,
splintered the photograph   lightning that no one saw
of lightning   striking earth,
                      blood vessels,
photo of splintered lightning   the shapes of rivers. creeks and

this is the ascent out of water:
there is no time but that
of convenience, tiny so that everything
weren't happen at once; dark
doesn't fall — dark comes up
out of the earth, an exhalation.

Pere Marquette
Pine
Hersey,
Manistee
Red Cedar
Boardman
Betsie
Platte
Sucker
Dragg
Omanogon
Escanaba
Yellowdog
Missouri
Mississippi
Yellowstone
Gallitin
Madison
Rio Grande
Rio de Chelly
Charles
Hudson
Pigeon
Black
Jordan
Rheux
Volga ?
Neva
Seine
Rio
Mobile
Snake
Bechler
Blue Nile
White Nile

It gathers itself close
to the ground, rising
to envelop us, as if the bottom
of the sea rose up to meet us.
♪ Have you ever gone
to the bottom of the sea? ♫

Mute unity of water.
I sculpted this girl
out of ice so beautifully
she was taken away.
How banal the siren song
which is a water song.
There never was a siren
who said goodbye. My raven
in the pine tree squawked his way
to death, falling from branch
to branch, to branch again,
to ground. The song, the muffle
of earth as the body falls.

. . .

Near the estuary north of Guilford
my brother recites the Episcopalian
burial service over his dead daughter.
Gloria, as in Gloria in excelsis
I cannot bear this passion and courage
and my eyes turn toward the swamp
and see, so blurred they can't quite
clear themselves again. The inside of the
vitreous humor is the same pulp found
inside the squid. I can see Gloria
on the snow and in the water. She lives
in the snow and water and I compose
songs for her. this is a song for her

teach me to type Joyce : check technical info

Kokopele saved me this time:
flute song in soft dark.
sound of water over rock,
the moon glitter rippling;
breath catches ~~caught~~ as my hunches
began moved in a ~~circles~~ coming,
eleven times around the cabin
through the ~~forest~~ woods in the dark.
Why did I decide to frighten myself.

. . .

~~the~~ coyote called back to the loon's
call perhaps for reasons of humor
light snow in early may,
wolf prints in alluvial fan moving
across a sand bar in the braided
river, ~~slipping into reeds and cattails~~ chords with me
~~I turn from the book (Oscar Wais)~~
~~to the tracks dozen times as if I had~~
~~discovered a new bird on earth.~~

then out of reed across the ice
~~& of~~ a dead channel, into the swamp.

" " o

The closest I came to describing it:
It is early winter, mid November.
with light snow, the ground rock hard
with frost. We are moving but I can't
seem to find my wife and two daughters.
I have left our old house and can't remember
how to find the new one.

. .

The days are stacked against
what we think we are:
the story of the water babies
swimming up and down stream
amid water-weed, twisting
with smiles in the current,
human and fish married.
Again! the girl I so painfully
sculpted out of ice
was taken away. She said:
"Goddamn the Lizard King,"
her night message and goodbye
the days are stacked against
what we think we are:
near the raven rookery   (chippewa's
inside the bend of river   ate babies
with snowmelt and rain   young raven
flooding the bend; I've failed   babies)
to stalk these birds again and they flutter
and wheel above me with parental screams
saying get out get out you bastard.
The days are stacked against
what we think we are:
after a month of interior weeping
it occurred to me in times like these
I have nothing to fall back on
except the sun and moon and earth.
I dress in camouflage and crawl
around swamps and forest, seeing
the bitch coyote five times but never
before she sees me. Her look
is curious; almost a smile.

The days are stacked against
what we think we are:
it is nearly impossible
to surprise ourselves.
I will never wake up
and be able to play the piano.
South still near fifteen miles, still
near the river, calling coyotes
with Dennis E: Full moon in east,
northern lights in pale green swirl,
from the west an immense snow squall
and thunderstorm approaching off Lake Superior.
Failing with his call he uses
the 'song of the loon' to bring
an answer from the coyotes.
"They can't resist it," he says.
The days are stacked against
what we are think we are.
Standing in the river up to my waist
the infant beaver peeks at me
from the flooded tag-alder
and approaches though warned
by his mother whacking her tail.
About seven feet away he bobs
to dive, mooning me with his small
pink ass, rising again for another
look, then downward, swimming
past my leg, still looking.
The days are finally stacked
against what we think we are:
how long can I stare at the river?
three months in a row now
with no signs of stopping,
glancing to the right, an almost

embarassed feeling that the river
will stop flowing and I can go home.
the days, at last, are stacked against
what we think we are.
Who in their most hallowed, sleepless
night with the moon seven feet
out side the window, the moon
that the river swallows would wish
it otherwise.

. . .

On New Years Eve I'm wrapped
in my habits, looking up to the TV
to see the red ball, the apple
rise or fall, I forget which:
a poem on the cherry wood fire,
a blizzard, some whiskey, three
restless cats, and two sleeping dogs.
at home and making three gallons
of menudo for the revelers who'll
need it come tomorrow after amateur night you need
about 10 pounds of tripe, ancho
molida, serrano, and chipotle peppers, cumin,
coriander, a few calves' or piglet feet.
I don't wonder what is becoming
to the man already becoming.
I also added a half quart of stock
left over from last nights bollito misto
wherein I poach for appropriate times:
fifteen pounds of veal bones to be discarded,
a beef brisket, a pork roast, italian sausage,
a large barnyard hen, a pheasant, a guinea
hen, and for about thirty minutes until
rosy rare a whole filet, served with
three sauces _____ , picante (anchovies & capers etc.)

and _____ . Last week after my daughter
came home from NYC I made her venison
with truffles, also roast quail for Christmas
breakfast, also some roast mallards & grouse,
(a wild turkey)
also a cacciatore of rabbit & pheasant.
Oddly the best meal of the year
was in the cabin by the river:
a single fresh brook trout "au bleu"
with one boiled new potato and one
wild leek vinaigrette. By the river
I try to keep alone, perhaps to write
more poems, though lately I think
of us all as lay-down comedians.
Who, when we finally get up,
have found that our feet are mushy,
and what is more, no one cares
or bothers to read anymore those
"sotto voce" below radar flights
from the empirical. But I am wrapped
in my habits. I must send my prayer
upward and downward. Why do you write
poems the stewardess asked. I guess
it's because every angel is terrible
still though, alas, I maybe there a more
deadly birds of the soul,
I cribbed from Rilke

. . .

He travels on dry riverbeds: Salt River.
Or Nearly dry, up canyon de chelly.
a half-foot of water - a skin over
the brown river bed, the Navajo
family stuck with a load of dry

corn and crabapples. Only the woman
speaks English, the children at first shy
and frightened of my blind, peggy left eye.
(some tribes attach importance to this -
strangely enough, it can see under water.
We're on the del Muerto fork and while
I'm kneeling in the water shoving rocks
under the axle I glance skywards
    at an Anasazi (sp) cliff dwelling, the "ancient
    ones" they're called. This morning
a young schizophrenic Navajo attacked
our truck with a club, his head seeming
to turn nearly all the way around as
an owl's. Finally the children smile -
the truck is pulled free. I am given
a hatfull of the most delicious crabapples
in the world. I watch the first apple
core float west on the slender current,
my throat a knot of everything
I no longer understand.

                    ✱ ✦ ✱

Sitting on the bank, the water
stares back so deeply you can hear
it afterwards when you wish. It is the water
of dreams, and for the nightwalker
who can almost walk on the water,
It is most of all the water of awakening,
passing with the speed of life
herself, drifting in circles in an eddy
joining again the current again
as if the eddy were a few moments' sleep

The story can't hesitate to stop.

~~the wild page~~

I can't find a river in Los Angeles
except the cement one behind Sportmen's Lodge
on Ventura. There I feel my
high blood pressure like an electric tiara
around my head, a small cosmic cloud,
a miniature junkyard where my confused
desires, hopes, hates and loves, short circuit
in little puffs of hissing ozone. And the women
as hard green horses disappearing,
concealing themselves in buildings and tops
of wild palms in ambush.
A riverless city of redolent
and banal sobs, green girls
in trees, girls hard as basalt
"My grandfather screwed me
when it was ~~such~~ ~~three~~ seven years old"
she said, while I looked out
    at the cement river flowing with dusty rain,
at three dogs playing in the cement river.
"He's dead now ~~and~~ there's no point
    sweating it," she added. ~~One of the dog's~~
~~fetched a drowned rat and the others chased~~

.   o   oo   o

Up in the amazon River basin
during a dark time Mathiessen built
a raft with a native, chewed some coca leaves,
boarded the raft and off they went on a river
not on any map, uncharted, wanting to see
the Great Molten of Snakes; a truncated
version of the your voyage of seventy years —
actual average. To see green and live green,
moving on water sometimes clouded often clear.
Now the water our own roads is white with ice
In the barnyard praying in the snow
you can hear the underground creek..
a creek without a name .

      * * *

I forgot to tell you that while
I was away my heart broke
and I became not so much old, but older,
definably older within a few days.
this happened one cold dawn in New Orleans
while I was feeding a frightened, stray
dog a sack of pork rinds in the cold rain.

      . . .

three girls danced the cotton-eyed Joe,
almost sedate, erect, with relentless grace,
Where did they come from
and where did they go
in ever so delicate circles?
and because of times, circles
that no long close
or return to themselves.

I rode the grey horse
all day in the rain.
The fields became unmoving rivers,
the trees foreshortened.
I saw a girl in a white dress
standing half hidden in the water
behind a maple tree
I pretended not to notice
and made a long slow circle
behind a floating hedge top
to catch her unawares.
She was gone but I had that prickly
fear someone was watching from a tree,
far up in a leaf-veil of green maple leaves.
Now the horse began swimming
toward higher ground, from where
I watched the tree until dark,
~~first taking off the bit so the horse could feed~~

See ? deletion
add Sept 9 "Tape"

"Is it terrible to be lonely and ill?"
she wrote. "Not at all, in fact, it is better
to be lonely when ill. To others, friends,
relatives, loved, ones, death is our most.
interesting, our most dramatic act.
Perhaps the best thing I've learned
from these apparently cursed and bedraggled
indians I've studied all these years
is how to die. Last year I sat beside
a seven year old Hopi girl as she sang
her death song in a slight quavering
voice. Who among us whites, child
or adult, will sing while we die?
You could, if you like, write something
for me to sing. I'm a scholar not a poet."

On White Fish Bay, the motor broke down
in heavy seas. We chopped ice off the gunwhales
quite happily as it was unlikely we'd survive
and it was something to do. Ted just sat there
out of the wind and spray drinking whiskey.
"I been on the wagon for a year. If I'm going
to die by god at least I get to have a drink.

. . .

What is it to actually go outside the nest
we have built for ourselves, and earlier
our father's nest : to go into a forest
alone with our eyes open? It's different
when you don't know what's over the hill —
keep the river on your left, then you see
the river on your right. I have simply
forgotten left an right, even up and down:
where and sleep on a cloudy day to forget
direction. It is hard to learn how
to be lost after so much training

. . .

In New York I clocked
seven tug boats on the East River
in less than a half hour,
then I went to a party
where very rich people
talked about their arches,
foot arches, not architectural arches.
Back at my post I dozed
and saw only one more tugboat
before a slept.

. .

. . .

But in New York I also saw a big hole
of maddened pipes with all the direction
of the swastika and a few immigrants
figuring it all out with the impenetrable
good sense of those who do the actual
work of the world:

. . .

How did I forget that rich turbulent
river, so cold in the rumply brown folds
of spring; by August cool, clear, glittery
in the sunlight; umbrous as it dips
under the logjam. In May, the river
a roar beyond a thin wall of sleep, with
the world of snow still gliding in rivulets
down imperceptible slopes; in August
through the screened window against with
bugs and moths scratch so lightly.
as lightly as the river sound.

. . .

How can I renew oaths
I can't quite remember?
In New Orleans I was light in body and soul
because of food poisoning, the bathroom gymnastics
of flesh against marble floor.
Seeing the underside of the bathtub
for the first time since I was a child.
And next day crossing Cajun bridges
in the Atchafalaya, where blacks were thrown
to alligators I'm told, black souls a-hurling
in brown water, whirling
in the immaculate crawfish rosary.

. . .

In the water I can remember
women I didn't know: Adriana
dancing her way home at the end
of a rope, a cool Tuscan night,
the apple tree in bloom;
the moon which I checked
was not quite full, a half-moon,
the rest of the life abandoned to the dark

. . .

All night I warned myself
but halfway between my ears
I turned toward the heavens,
and reached the top of my head.
From there I can go just about
anywhere I want and I've never
found my way back home.

. . .

This isn't the old song
of the suicidal house,
I forgot the tune about small
windows growing smaller, the
door neither big enough to enter
or exit, the hydraulic ceilings
and the attic full of wet cement.
~~I batted through a wall and went to Corsica,~~
~~returned the next morning feeling better.~~
I wanted to go to the Camargue,
to Corsica, to return to Costa Rica
but I couldn't escape the suicidal house
~~house~~ until may when I drove
through the snow to reach the river.

. . .

On the bank by the spring creek
my shadow seemed to leap
up to gather me, or it leapt
up to gather me, not seeming so
but as a natural fact. Faulkner said
that the drowned man's shadow had watched
him from the river all the time.

. . .

Drowning in the bourgeois trough,
a bourride or gruel of money, drugs,
whiskey, hotels, the dream coasts,
ass in air at the trough, drowning
in a river of pus, pus of civilization.
pus of cities, unholy river of shit,
of filth, shit of nightmares, shit
of skewed dreams and swallowed years.
the river pulls me out,
  draws me elsewhere
  and down to blue water,
    green water,
      black water.

. . .

How far between the Virgin
and the Garrison and back?
Why is it a hundred times further to get back,
the return upriver in the dark.
  It isn't innocence but to win back breath,
body heat, the light that gathers around
  a waking animal. Ten years ago I saw
the dancing Virgin in a basement
  in New York, a whirl of hot color
from floor to ceiling, whirling in a dance

At eighteen in New York City
on Grove Street I discovered
red wine, garlic and, Rimbaud,
and a red haired girl. Sand colors
not known in farm country,
also Sonny Rollins, Charlie Parker:
the odors from restaurant vents.
thirty-five cent italian sausages
on MacDougald, and the Hudson River.
Days of river watching and trying
to get on a boat for the tropics and see
that great ocean river, the gulf stream
another fifteen years before I saw
the ocean reefs and the sharks hanging
under the saragassum weed ledges,
a blue river in green water,
and the sharks slowing back, sinking
down listlessly into darker water

I'm drawing this picture as a child
draws a picture, explaining it's either
a picture of the world, or a bear falling
out of the sky if an electric fence.
the world needs bears as much as posts

Where did I hear that poems
are written to waken sleeping gods;
these gods don't get around much anymore.
or have taken on nearly unrecognizable
forms as gods will do: one is a dog.
one is a scarecrow that doesn't work -
crows perch on the wind-whipped sleeves;
one is a carpenter who doesn't become Jesus,
one was a girl who went to heaven
sixty years early. Gods die.
and not always out of choice, like cats near-sighted
jumping between building, seven
stories up. On certain days we awaken
as gods and forget by breakfast,
or when the phone rings. Many doubt
that they are there

Start here

I forget when I heard that poems
Where did I hear that poems
are designed to waken sleeping gods;
in our time they've taken on nearly
unrecognizable shapes as gods will do:
one is a dog, one is a scarecrow
that doesn't work - crows perch
on the wind-whipped sleeves,
one is a carpenter who doesn't become Jesus,
one is a girl who went to heaven
sixty years early. Gods die,
and not always out of choice,
like near-sighted cats jumping
between buildings seven stories up.
I never drew feathers out of my skin
so I could fly, a favor close to terror.

But This isn't a map of the gods.
When they live in rivers
it's because rivers have no equilibrium;
gods resent equilibrium when everything
that lives, "moves," ~~when~~ Boulders
are a way of atoms, and the dandelion
cracks upward through the blacktop road.
Seltzer's tropical beetle grew
from a larval lump in ~~an~~ man's arm,
emerging full grown, pincers waving.
On Mt. Cuchama there were ~~too~~ many
gods passing through one day.
I hid in a hole in ~~the~~ the rock
and wakened one ~~day~~ ~~I wasn't ready~~
and walked ~~away~~ with a light ass
and cold skin. I could draw a map
but have never found one in the same place
twice. And their voices change from involuntary
screams to the singular wail of the loon,
possibly the wind that I feel howl down Wall St.
Gods have long abandoned the banality of war
though they were stirred by a hundred year old
guitarist I heard in Brazil, & the autistic child
at the piano. We'll be greeted at death
~~but why should I wait that long~~. Today I invoked
any available god back in the woods in the fog.
The world was white with last week's melting
blizzard, the fog drifting upward, then descending
the only sound was a porcupine eating bark
off an old tree, and a rivulet beneath the snow.
Sometimes the obvious is true: the full
moon on her bare bottom by the river!
For the gay, the full moon on the lover's prick.
Gods laugh at the fiction of gender

Water gods, moon gods, ~~god fever~~ sun gods fire gods,
open my mouth, give me ~~more~~ songs before I die.
~~give this earth ever~~

★ check notebook   . . .   channel morphology

It is hard for some to imagine a man
growing ~~old~~ with eagerness

the "system" suggests the cutting off,
i.e., in channel morphology, the reductive,
the suppression of texture to simplify:
to understand a man, or woman, growing
old with eagerness you first consider
the sensuality of death, an unacknowledged
surprise to most. In nature the physiology
has heat and color, beast and tree
saying aloud the wonder of death
to study rivers, including the ~~banality~~ postcard
of waterfalls, is to adopt another life;
a limited life attaches itself to the endless
movement ⅔ the renowned underground
rivers of South America which I've felt
thundering far beneath my feet. To die
is to descend into such rivers flowing
along in the ~~dark~~ perfect dark. But above ground
I'm memorizing life from the winter moon
to the sound of my exhaustion in March
when all the sodden plans have collapsed
and only daughters, the dogs and cats
keep ~~one~~ from disappearing at gunpoint.
I brought myself here and stare nose to nose
at the tolerant cat who laps whiskey, shakes ?
from my moustache. at an exact moment she Life often shatters
in schizoid splinters. I watch this I well armed
~~betraying the cold stone wall~~ I am shuddering
~~straddling a cold stone wall~~

I had forgot what it was I liked
about life. I hear if you own a chimpanzee
they cease at a point to be funny. Writers
and politicians share an embarassed moment
when they are sure all problems will disappear
if you get the language just right.
That's not all they share — in each other's
company they are like boys who have been
discovered at weiner play in the toilet.
At worst, it's the gift of gab.
At best it's Martin Luther King and Rimbaud.
Bearing down hard on love and death
there is an equal and opposite reaction.
All these years they have split the pie
leaving the topping for preachers
who don't want folks to fuck or eat.
What kind of magic, rite of fertility
to transcend this shit-soaked stew?

The river is as far as I can move
from the world of numbers: I'm all
for full retreats, escapes, a 47 yr old runaway.
"Hitler's too old to run away" I wrote
but not quite believing this option is grey.
I stare into the deepest pool of the river
which holds the mystery of a cellar to a child:
and think of those two track roads that dwindle
into nothing in the forest. I have this feeling
of walking around for years with the wind
knocked out of me. In the cellar was a root
cellar where we stored potatoes, apples, carrots
and where a family of harmless black snakes lived.
In certain rivers there are pools a hundred
foot deep. In a swamp I must keep secret
there is a deep boiling spring around which
in the dog days of August large brook trout
swim and feed. An adult can speak dreams
to children saying that there is a spring
that goes down to the center of the earth.
Maybe there is. Next summer I'm designing
and building a small river about seventy-seven
foot long. It will flow both ways, in reverse
of nature. I will build a dam and blow it up.

The involuntary image that sweeps
into the mind, irresistible and without evident
cause as a dream or thunderstorm,
or rising to the surface from childhood,
the longest journey taken in a split-second;
from there to now, without pause:
in the woods with Mary Cooper, my first love
wearing a violet scarf in May. We're
looking after her huge mongoloid aunt,
trailing after this woman who loves us,
but so dimly perceives the world. We pick
dirt
and clean wild leeks for her. The creek
is wild and dangerous with the last
of the snow melt. The child-woman
tries to enter the creek and we tackle her.
She's stronger than slowly understands,
half-wet and muddy. She kisses me
while Mary laughs then Mary kisses me
over and over. Now I see the pools
in the Mongol eyes that watch and smile
with delight and hear the roar of the creek,
smell the scent of leeks on her muddy lips.

This is ~~the~~ ~~pornographic~~ an "obscene" Koan set plumb
in the middle of the Occident:
the man with three hands lacks symmetry
but claps the loudest, the chicken
in circles on the sideless road, a plane
that takes off and can never land.
I am not quite alert enough to live.
The fallen nest and fire in the closet,
my world without guardrails, the electric
noose , the puddle that had no bottom.
The fish in underground rivers are white
and blind as the porpoises far up who live
the muddy Amazon. In ~~many places~~ K and p A
now you don't want to see, or hear or smell
and you open your mouth only in restaurants,
but you can touch anyone without soft hard skin?
I'm trying to become alert enough to live.
Yesterday after the blizzard I hiked far back
in a new swamp and found an iceless
pond connected to the river by a small creek.
Against deep white snow and black trees
there was a sulphrous fumarole, rank and shady
in cold air. The water bubbled up brown,
then spread in turquoise to black
without the track of single mammal to drink—
this was nature's own, a beauty too strong
for life; a place to drown not live.

On waking after the accident
I was presented with the "whole picture"
of life on earth, magnificently detailed,
a childs diorama of what life appears to be:
staring at the picture I became drowsy
with sweet relief when I noticed a yellow
dot of light in the lower right-hand corner.
I unhooked the machines and tubes and crawled
to the picture, with an eyeball to the dot
of light which turned out to be a miniature
tunnel at the end of which I could see
mountains and stars whirling and tumbling
sheets of emotions, vertical rivers,
lakes, herds of unknown mammals,
the bottom of Isaiah's robe, live whales
on dry ground, lions drinking from a golden
bowl of milk, the rush of night,
and somewhere in this, the murmur of gods—
a tree-rubbing-tree music, a sweet howl
of water and rock grating rock, fire
hissing from fissures, the moon settled
comfortably on the ground, beginning to roll.

ABOUT THE AUTHOR

Over a fifty-year writing career, Jim Harrison (1937–2016) published nearly forty books of poetry, fiction, and nonfiction, all of which remain in print. His work has been translated into two dozen languages. Harrison is widely credited with reviving the novella form with the publication of the trilogy *Legends of the Fall.* The success of *Legends* led to his work in Hollywood writing screenplays. Known also for his deep appreciation for food and drink, Harrison wrote popular food columns for several journals and magazines, notably *Brick* and *Esquire.* In 2007 he was elected to the American Academy of Arts and Letters, and his extensive literary archive is housed at Grand Valley State University.

Jim Harrison was fiercely loyal to independent publishers, and two independent publishers are particularly loyal to his work: Grove Atlantic is dedicated to publishing Harrison's fiction and nonfiction, and Copper Canyon Press is committed to his poetry.

As the *Sunday Times* (London) wrote, "Jim Harrison is a writer with immortality in him."

ABOUT THE EDITOR

Joseph Bednarik was the co-publisher and marketing director of Copper Canyon Press. He has served as Jim Harrison's poetry editor since the late 1990s.

ABOUT THE CONTRIBUTOR

Writer, historian, and activist Rebecca Solnit is the author of more than twenty books on feminism, Western and urban history, popular power, social change and insurrection, wandering and walking, hope and catastrophe. Her books include *Orwell's Roses, Recollections of My Nonexistence,* and *Men Explain Things to Me.*

THE HEART'S WORK:
JIM HARRISON'S POETIC LEGACY

The mission of The Heart's Work is to secure and advance Jim Harrison's legacy as a poet, and to keep Jim's poems in wide and ever-growing circulation. The following visionaries deserve special recognition because they answered *yes* when we asked for help at the outset:

Special thanks to the generous writers who provided introductions and afterwords to volumes published as part of The Heart's Work:

Denver Butson

John Freeman

Ted Kooser

Colum McCann

Naomi Shihab Nye

Rebecca Solnit

Joy Williams

Terry Tempest Williams

Copper Canyon Press thanks the following supporters of The Heart's Work. Each and all have helped bring this new edition of *The Theory & Practice of Rivers* to life:

Anonymous

Porter Abbott

Ginny Agnew

Cameron Alexander

Blaine Allan

Richard Anderson

Virginia Anderson

Loretta Libby Atkins
and Martha Jo Trolin

Adam F. Bailey

Ryan W. Bailey

Lynne Bannerman

Yves C.L. Barbeau

Craig Barfoot

Mike Baron

Hathaway Barry

Molly Bauer

Jake Benes

Peter David Birt

Wolfe Blotzer

Will Blythe

Zackry Bodine

Joseph Branch

David Brewster and
Mary Kay Sneeringer

Deborah Buchanan and
Scott Teitsworth

Vincent T. Buck

Dan Burns and
Lorraine Diaz

Michael Butler

Christine Campadieu

Arnold Blaine
Campbell

David Capers

Susan Carkin

Tom Carney

F. Carsey

Sarah J. Cavanaugh

Christopher Chaffee

Chad M. Christensen

Mark Christopherson

Harriett Cody and
Harvey Sadis

Mark Cohen

Nancy V. Colahan

Elizabeth J. Coleman
and Robert Stroup

Mary L. Collins

Coley, Kati, and Mike
Conklin

Clyde (Sandy) Crancer

Art Curtis

Jerry Davis

Seabring and Colin
Davis

Michael Delp, a.k.a.
The Mad Angler

Robert DeMott and
Kate Fox

Ian Demsky

Hank Dickinson and
June Moon

Ron Domen

Elizabeth Doran

Martin Dudley

Drew Dumsch and Lisa
Farago

Mary and John
("Nick") Dumsch

Danny Dunphy Jr.

Renee DuSoleil

Rhae Eaton

David J. Edney

Ted Efstratis

John Albert Ehrenfried

The Evans Family

Dan Fahrbach

Patricia Farmer

Mary Kay Feather

Mark A. Ferguson

Michael Ferreboeuf

Beroz Ferrell of The Point, LLC

Ross A. Field

David C. Flask

Tom and Tamara Foley

Julie Fowler

Rocky Friedman

Friends at Square Books

Mike Frost

Andreana Gamache

Loretta Gase

Annie and Rick Gordon

David and Pamela Grath

Great Basin Water Network

Harry Greene

Robert Greenwood

Miles Dean Grussing

Andrew Haley

Jim Halligan

Art Hanlon

Daniel J. Harrington

David and Cynthia Harrison

John Hawkinson

Tom Hight

Jack Hill

Stephen Hill

Dave Himber

Thomas A. Hinds

Carol Jane Hoover

Steven Hopkins

Judy Hottensen

Holly J. Hughes and John Pierce

Cliff Hume

Peg Hunter and Patrick Johnson

Susan Jackson

Ninon Jamet

Steven Johnston

Daniel and Katherine Jones

Bruce S. Kahn

George Kalamaras

Lyle S. Kearns

Joseph Edmund Kelly

Matthew Boyce Kelly

Patrick G. Kessel

Alexandra Guequierre Klodenski

Taroh Kogure

Kim Kopetz

Tom Lakin

Chris La Tray

Christopher Lawson

Caroline Livermore

Kevin and Cristin Lyons

Marie Marchand

Catherine Marchiando

In honor of Ron Martin-Dent, my son

Larry Mawby and Lois Bahle

David Ira Mayberg

Andrew Douglas McCallum

Terry McDonell and Stacey Hadash

Joel Mitchell

Jorge Monteiro

Charles Morgan

Elizabeth Douglas Mornin

Joseph P. Morra

Jay Morris, MD

Joan L. Murphy

In honor of Julia Elena Musto

Brett Navin

John Nettleton and Bryan Hathaway

Bill Newton

Jennifer and Jamie Newton

Derbyshire Nikkels

Vergil E. Noble

Rick Bear OConnell, Carissa Lee OConnell, and dogs Nalu and Koa

Mary Oehl-Huinker

Priscilla Oppenheimer

Sharon L. Oriel

Gregg Orr

H.C. and Valerie Palmer

Greg Pape

Patric A. Parker

Stewart Parker

Walter Parsons

Barney Sue Fife Patterson Peacock

Ben J. Peacock

Brian Perry

Marc Petrie
Mark Phillips
Shawn and Kathrine
    Pittard
Richard S. Posey
P.M. Rankin
Shann Ray
Dan Raymond
Allyson Rennell
Lou Reynolds
Patricia Richardson
Larry Ridley
Sara and Tripp Ritter
Tod F. Roach
Thomas A. Robison
Bethany M. Rodenhuis
Ramiro Rodriguez
Marc Rosen
John P. Rosenberg
Jeffery David Ross
Shelli Rottschafer and
    Daniel Combs
Michael Running

Richard M. Russell
Pamela Jean Sampel
Dean Schabner
Jeffrey and Lea Scherer
Kim and Jeff Seely
Chris Shafer
Barbara Brattin Siler
Robert A. Simpson, MD
G. Mark Skinner
Randall Steven Smith
Gwendolyn and Stan
    Soper
Dino Sparaco
Stephen Spencer
Scott Owen Sprunger
Tait Stamp
In memory of Clemens
    Starck
Joan Strassmann and
    David Queller
Yolanda Danyi Szuch
John Michael
    Tanzine IV
Keith Taylor

Ron and Gail Trendler
Gregg Trexler
Chase Twichell
Jeffrey Utzinger
Claudia Valentino
Linda Walsh and Keith
    Cowan
Aub Ward, in memory
    of Grayson Ward
Doug Wick and Lucy
    Fisher
Marilyn Wolf
Dar Wolnik
Joan Woods
Wes Yard
Robert Yeakle
Glen and Jane Young
Jeff Zillgitt and Alison
    Maxwell
Guy and Mary
    Zimmerman

Poets for Poetry

Copper Canyon Press poets are at the center of all our efforts as a nonprofit publisher. Poets not only create the art that defines our books, but they read and teach the books we publish. Many are also generous donors who believe in financially supporting the larger poetry community of Copper Canyon Press. For decades, our poets have quietly donated their royalties, have directly engaged in our fundraising campaigns, and have made personal donations in support of the next generation. Their support has encouraged the innovative risk-taking that sustains and furthers the art form.

The donor-poets who have contributed to the Press since 2023 include:

Jonathan Aaron
Kelli Russell Agodon
Pamela Alexander
Joyce Harrington Bahle
Ellen Bass
Mark Bibbins
Sherwin Bitsui
Marianne Boruch
Laure-Anne Bosselaar
Cyrus Cassells
Peter Cole and Adina Hoffman
Elizabeth J. Coleman
John Freeman
Forrest Gander
Jenny George
Daniel Gerber
Julian Gewirtz
Jorie Graham
Robert and Carolyn Hedin
Bob Hicok
Ha Jin
Jaan Kaplinski
Laura Kasischke

Jennifer L. Knox
Ted Kooser
Deborah Landau
Sung-Il Lee
Ben Lerner
Dana Levin
Heather McHugh
Jane Miller
Lisa Olstein
Gregory Orr
Eric Pankey
Kevin Prufer
Paisley Rekdal
James Richardson
Alberto Ríos
David Romtvedt
Natalie Shapero
Arthur Sze
Elaine Terranova
Chase Twichell
Ocean Vuong
Connie Wanek-Dentinger
Emily Warn

Poetry is vital to language and living. Since 1972, Copper Canyon Press has published extraordinary poetry from around the world to engage the imaginations and intellects of readers, writers, booksellers, librarians, teachers, students, and donors.

WE ARE GRATEFUL FOR THE MAJOR SUPPORT PROVIDED BY:

academy of
american poets

A&
OFFICE OF ARTS & CULTURE
SEATTLE

ARTSFUND

THE PAUL G. ALLEN
FAMILY FOUNDATION

Hawthornden
Foundation

PO
ET
RY
FOUNDATION

INGRAM
CONTENT GROUP

the point
envision·enact·evolve

McSWEENEY'S

WASHINGTON STATE
ARTS COMMISSION

ART WORKS.
National
Endowment
for the Arts
arts.gov

The Witter Bynner Foundation
for Poetry

TO LEARN MORE ABOUT UNDERWRITING
COPPER CANYON PRESS TITLES,
PLEASE CALL 360-385-4925 EXT. 105

WE ARE GRATEFUL FOR THE MAJOR SUPPORT PROVIDED BY:

Anonymous

Jill Baker and Jeffrey Bishop

Anne and Geoffrey Barker

Donna Bellew

Lisha Bian

Will Blythe

John Branch

Diana Broze

John R. Cahill

Sarah J. Cavanaugh

Keith Cowan and Linda Walsh

Peter Currie

Geralyn White Dreyfous

The Evans Family

Mimi Gardner Gates

Gull Industries Inc.
   on behalf of William True

Carolyn and Robert Hedin

David and Jane Hibbard

Bruce S. Kahn

Phil Kovacevich and Eric Wechsler

Maureen Lee and Mark Busto

Ellie Mathews and Carl Youngmann
   as The North Press

Larry Mawby and Lois Bahle

Petunia Charitable Fund and
   adviser Elizabeth Hebert

Suzanne Rapp and Mark Hamilton

Adam and Lynn Rauch

Emily and Dan Raymond

Joseph C. Roberts

Cynthia Sears

Kim and Jeff Seely

Tree Swenson

Julia Sze

Barbara and Charles Wright

In honor of C.D. Wright
   from Forrest Gander

Caleb Young as C. Young Creative

The dedicated interns and faithful
   volunteers of Copper Canyon Press

The pressmark for Copper Canyon Press
suggests entrance, connection, and interaction
while holding at its center
an attentive, dynamic space for poetry.

This book is set in LTC Deepdene.
Book design by Gopa & Ted2, Inc.
Printed in Canada on archival-quality paper.